The author's poetry is by design. The Almighty has shown His favour on her. It is obvious that there is a divine connection, this can only lead into greater deeds for the Master. I truly read with interest each poem and I chuckle at some of the titles especially Flying Pigs. It is her testimony and I have every reason to believe that this would help in introducing the readers. I see this book of poetry as an asset to Women's conferences and gatherings. Lady Poet, may you continue to grow where you are planted and blessings always.

Dr Pamela Appelt- Citizenship
Retired Judge-: Court of Canadian Citizenship
Artist

An indelible spiritual watermark, on the tapestry of this divinely inspired poetic journey, is the prayer of St. Francis that is resonating, validating and accompanying the soundings of the author's heart. The soundings of the resolute heart to live life: From the heart and the mind; from the body-soul and the soul-body; from the divine-human and the human-divine; with the light in the darkness and the darkness in the light; in the beauty from the ugly through the duty and the drudgery. These poetic lines. It is in dying to self that we are born to eternal life.

Fr. Kenneth Assing
Archdiocese of Port of Spain
Trinidad and Tobago

What is 'the road less travelled by',
what can make 'pigs to fly',
and what can heal a broken heart?
It is the word, the thought the rhyme of love.
It is the Master's touch, His still, small voice,
the promise not forgotten
and that, ' has made all the difference'.
I commend to you this book of poems,
skillfully crafted from the journey of life.
May it be to you a blessing.

Reverend Canon Kim Beard
St. Paul's on the Hill Anglican Church, Pickering.

"Thank you for your poetry. I feel your inspiration, your joy in the Lord".

George Elliott Clarke
Poet Laureate Toronto 2012-2015

"I made a painting last night, partly inspired by *In Changing Seasons*. It says «Sea fuerte en mente, cuerpo, corazón y espíritu toda la vida». Which literally translates: *to be strong in mind, body, heart and soul all through life*. I am reminded that in addition to taking care of our physical and mental health, we also have to remember to nourish ourselves spiritually and emotionally. The changing seasons (fall) is meant to contrast and also complement because on the one hand, you want to remain strong despite all the change around, but also, you don't want to remain unchanged or else you have not grown/learned... So you see, it's open to interpretation".

Tracy Torres
BA Psycholinguistics- University of Toronto, Scarborough

Inspiring Words
as Your World Turns

In
Changing
Seasons

Jo Anne C. Blackman

Printed in Canada

ISBN: 978-1-4866-0938-3

Word Alive Press
131 Cordite Road, Winnipeg, MB R3W 1S1
www.wordalivepress.ca

Library and Archives Canada Cataloguing in Publication

Blackman, Jo Anne C., 1964-, author
   In changing seasons : inspiring words as your world
turns / Jo Anne C. Blackman.

Poems.
Issued in print and electronic formats.
ISBN 978-1-4866-0938-3 (paperback).--ISBN 978-1-4866-0939-0
(pdf).--ISBN 978-1-4866-0940-6 (html).--ISBN 978-1-4866-0941-3
(epub)

   1. Christian poetry, Canadian (English). I. Title.

PS8603.L273I6 2015   C811'.6   C2015-904569-X
                        C2015-904570-3

I dedicate *In Changing Seasons* to my mother.

Mommy, you have encouraged me to stand tall,
reminded me that God is always with me
no matter how far I travel from home,
He lives in me. Knowing and believing this
has kept me. You have been an incredible
example to me and I admire your steadfast
qualities.
Thank you Mommy, for all your prayers for
me and for my family over the years. And I know
what your reply to this dedication would be...

All the Glory to God...It Is He!

Introduction

IN JANUARY OF 1980- THE 18TH DAY, THE YEAR IN WHICH my father passed, I sat in my room and quietly sketched a few pictures. I had no real purpose for doing so, nor knowledge of what it all meant, but managed to keep them all this time. I had actually given them to my daughter on her sixteenth birthday. My father, having been diagnosed with a terminal illness some time before, would be called home at the end of March. I think it is wonderful that three of these pictures find a perfect place and true purpose as the section pages in my book.

The first half of my poems written, were inspirational based, though not intentionally. At my computer, awaiting news sometime in the middle of August 2014, my thoughts unexpectedly unravelled and were transcribed into black and white, day after day. Nearing the end of September 2014. I had written over 200 poems.

Many suggestions came from my niece Tracy, who challenged me to expand into different topics. She would say "write one about a lighthouse", then came *Go Beacon Go*, "about a jetty" and *Heading Home*, showed up.

Thank you to my dear family and wonderful friends who listened to endless hours of rhymes supporting and cheering me along. To the clergy and congregation at St Paul's on-the-Hill, who fanned the flame in me and of course to my Small Group, thank you so much. To the kind hearts, who graciously agreed to read these poems and dared to comment and provide advice. Remembering my editor Tracy Torres and to my publisher, most sincere blessings to you all.

If the title of my book was any other, it could have been "Flying Pigs". Unusual yes. I say this because Flying Pigs is a story of hope. Living in hope for me is living with the expectation of God being faithful to His promises: The Rock on which we stand. In Changing Seasons, the poem was the foundation on which the others that followed were built and the reason I selected to use it as the title.

We all have the making of a good Christian, as we have all fallen short of His glory, creating the opportunity for us to depend upon His grace to re-create us.

Live in hope, knowing that God is faithful to His promises. Listen to His calling. Seek His favour and place your trust in Him. Place Him first. "I love you" says the Lord.

This is my living message, my loving message for your kind consideration.

Jo Anne C. Blackman
Friend of God

Table of Contents

SECTION ONE - Keep Your Eyes On Me

SECTION TWO - Encouragement Galore

SECTION THREE - Hope

Section One

Keep Your Eyes On Me

In Changing Seasons

In changing seasons
Of life events
When surprisingly they unfold
To remain unchanged and constant
In our attitudes
We are told
Standing firmly on the Rock
We sustain
No matter what

Giving Glory to our Creator

The temptation is great, it cannot be underscored
To write and write more about my Lord
How He enters my mind
and nibbles my fingers
Flows through my thoughts
and enables my thinking
On the computer
Then lies a new poem sometime later
Giving glory to our Creator

Mostly in rhymes He has given my style
Rarely planned by me, it just sounds out naturally
And when I write it seems as if I had written it before
So I review and re-read and add some more
You can do this, I know you can,
saying this to anyone
Prepares them to understand
That you believe it can be done

Thank you to all the believers
Your words were powerful
To write encouraging others
would be my privilege
My pleasure
Holding true to a standard of goodness
As grace dictates
Though it may not appear perfect
Trusting God for the message to relay

A Bag of Prayers

I know I should be praying for others
But I feel that there is so much I need
Not just me, but my immediate family

And as fast as I lift one up for blessings
No sooner does another come calling
Do you see, what's happening to me

There is my spouse and my children
On my job, the job, the boss, their boss
I can't afford to leave anyone out, a loss

Then my mom, my dad, my siblings too
Is there someone praying for you
Or do I, have to make time too

What of the wide world with much unjust
Is a prayer for all those a must
How do I decide about this list

I say Lord all knowing, You have this
A bag of prayers, my list

JO ANNE C. BLACKMAN

A Season to Enjoy

To be alive and live through each day
Relishing every moment's call
Hoping to soak up all and all
Still longing for yet another day
In which to stay

To share and be shared with, what joy
To belong, wrapped,
like one string a strand on the rope
With no isolation, no alone
Or a link on a chain, clinging to the others
Supporting with all that matters
Bonding and strengthening remaining together

To love and hold hands, what happiness
Living in kindness
Like a feather's brushing, a birdie's chirping
A gentle breeze blowing
Happiest then, like a river without an end
In finding His hand

In Obedience

Lord, I am hanging on in suspense
Even frozen at times
Needing that push, needing that fall
That fall, into your will

Steady me now, put my feet on the ground
And though I cannot seem to yet foresee
Your master plan for me
You tell me Lord
With Your messages scrolling out ahead of me

And I shall stand in obedience
In firm agreement
With that which is true and real
Symphony joining, Your conducting
In Christ my Lord

JO ANNE C. BLACKMAN

The Road We Travel

Birds of a feather for sure
Like talking the same language
demonstrating
An empathy, a common understanding
All because of the road we travel

In an upside down world with enough tidal waves
Constantly breaking and crashing
hearts churning
All across lands and islands too
Remains, Samaritan like mirroring

What then, is this road, this travel
I humbly propose
obedience
True followers loving the Father
Through the love for our neighbour

Walking in His footsteps
It is......the road we travel

And My Household Too

You are in control oh Lord my God
You know where I ought to be
Test me and find me worthy
For You have mapped my journey
And set me free

Help me to trust in Your ever faithful ways
Turning to You all of my days
Empty me of the old
So that I may receive all of You
And be renewed

Keep me forever, don't let me go
Let me turn to You for all my desires
Sanctify my heart, purify my soul
That I may cling to Your promises
And Your love

Cover me Lord, Keep me safe
With Your Angels all around me
Take my hands, my everything and lead me
To live a life of grace and goodness
And see Your face

JO ANNE C. BLACKMAN

Locust Eating Away

Tunnel or space
Confined or out of place
What is your phobia

Why are you not assured
Why do you quake
Why too, do you not exemplify

What does lie
Lie in your heart
Is it not strength, is it not faith

What is your phobia
Why do you quake
What does lie

Lie to you
And hold you in chains
The fear of the unknown

Unknown to you
But like the locust, eating away
Soon this phase, shall pass too

To look back
And be assured
Your path, in Him secured

As You Are

Come now, as you are
Don't worry, your state is of no matter
As for me, I would prefer to have you here
I know your thoughts, you are sorry
You can, run into my arms, come

I'll meet you where you are
Don't worry, don't wait any longer
All the while I have been towing your line
Awaiting your arrival from time
Yes, come

My life I did not spare
Because of you, how much I care
To be with me
In true freedom, freedom to and freedom from
Into my embracing arms, come

Be the Master of My Life

Thank You heavenly Lord, for all of my days my life
For teaching me how to place You first in my life
My true love
Let me remain forever grateful giving glory to God
Upon my heart, stitch Your Word and reside too
Bless me with Your holiness to live for You

Guide my steps gentle Jesus
That I may walk ever so closely with You
You in me and me in You
That during the storms in my life, You will prevail
Jesus, Lion of Judah, Saviour of the world
and of my soul
Creator, God
Glory to You Lord, let Your name be praised forever

Take charge of me Holy Spirit, emotions and all
Fight my fights with me, be present every second
With You as master, victory is won
By the cross it was done
So long ago before my time
You gave Your all in advance, so should I, so should I

Believe

Trouble pours down
Rise inner man
Take back yourself with Him strong
Born was He who died for us
To live a life as conquerors....believe

We are the temples of the Lord
His vessels, His receptacles
Let Him build us up
Keeping us kindled
To withstand all obstacles where they lay
Fire burning to stay....believe

Choice

Weak with him, strong with You
Whom shall I choose, which way do I steer
Must I really choose

Feel sad with him, happy with You
Uptight, can't do anything right
And with You, well, I am a light

Worse then, down and blue
You pull me up to see You
The choice is clear, here too

Why should I choose one or the other
Can't it be both of you
What will it take, for this to make

To make any sense of this matter
Fix it please, that it pleases You.
Loving Master

A Compass for You

Look to me for travelling
Suffer I beg, in obedience stay
Take my arrow as your own
Following the point, keeping me close
In your heart's pocket, I'll lead you home

If you look for direction, I will guide
Left or right you may start
But for light, look to the north
Though for a while, south you choose
Still, I'll show up just for you

Your travel, your choice
But know, through my eyes, I see my apple
My child, and longing for you to follow
Wanting the best for you
This is my gift to you, Christ

The Golden Rooms

When I step in, only then would I have arrived
Truly will I see, all that was meant to be
Golden rooms, grand and safe
Where too
I will meet those who kept the faith

Unimaginable, brighter than any, better than all
It shall compensate, like water into wine
The crucifixion, the cross, a reminder, a sign
Of His promise written
In John 14

Out of this world, truly I cannot even begin
To contemplate of the purity that exists
With solemn or vibrant worship as He wishes
Together with
The Father Son and Holy Spirit

Coming to Shore

Waves coming to shore
As if to rest in delight
Ups and downs, no more
Now another life, instead stretched out

As we re-learn and re-adjust
Before taken
And brought back, with
Each new tide

Yawning and stretching in relax
Horizontally, peacefully, almost to lay
Strength for a new day's surf
Our return, work or play

Bless our days
And restful nights, thank you for
Our coming back to shore
And being renewed by Your light

Evergreen Love

Love, like the evergreen band
Knowing exactly where it stands
Constant and unchanging
Except for stronger growing

Though powerful winds against you blow
Your love for each other still flows
And even though equal
Giving more than taking
Always remaining ever loving

Ever staying as decided
As on that first day when created
Decided and made out of love
Now you choose, to remain forever in love

Whatever comes your way, in storm or play
You are well prepared, you integrity in gear
Your roots cling to a particular way
Your thoughts are prompted to think as Jesus did
You think love, you think forgive

I Promise

You shall get through it
The sun rises each day, I was told do not dismay
Do not be discouraged, His promises are true
Have faith and always pray

Brother, you were right, Sister, you too
And the promise of our little one
"I promise", to me he said
"The sun will come out for you"

Forgiven

Yes, I have forgiven, Oh really
Then why do I bring it up, even daily
Leave it all at the foot of the cross
Do this daily instead, before more time is lost

Okay, this time I did it, Oh truly
Then why aren't you speaking really
Vexed and angry, thinking of yourself
Of why and how come
Remember, He has forgiven, it is done

Alright, I have this, or is it that He has me
Under His umbrella, His shelter mighty
Decide to follow Him and you will see
That who you were, can no longer be

Yes, He has forgiven me
Really, truly
So I accept this gift and His great mercy
Now all good things begin
Wishing goodwill to all, for who is without sin

Genie

Consider the love and adoration
Genie has for her master
Longing to please him
And no other, for she worries
That doing wrong will hurt him so deeply
She carefully reconsiders all her actions
Even when tempted, she talks out the consequences
And always comes to one conclusion
Pleasing her master is her first priority
Should we be more like Genie....

———————

Master, you touched me, saved me
I say, now I see your work in me
...I accept your love and restore

Master, let me please you
Out of gratitude, out of all
...I do everything, as you command me to

For my Master only
Granting His wish, shall I perform
...For only through Him, do I do any

In His Presence

I am in the presence of our Lord
Created in His image
To be like Him, holy
Though human am I, still I can be like Him, through
Him

I walk in the presence of our Lord
For He sent His only son
So that we can call on Him
Though human are we, still we can be like Him,
through Him

I breathe in the presence of our Lord
For His spirit is in me
It is the I AM in me
I can truly serve Him when I am in His presence

I live in the presence of our Lord
To love one another is to serve Him
To forgive one another is to love Him
His example is unconditional and perfect as He is

Only through Him and with Him, In His presence

His Rhythm, His Beat

Set your timer to His, your rhythm to His
Move with Him, to His call, to His beat
Don't even glance back, it will only delay a good
thing
The you, you should be, the turning, the happening

Listen only to Him, everything else off
Be silent, hush now, you don't want to miss out
And when you do speak, ask for mercy and peace
Grace too, to keep up with His pace

Clothe yourself in His garments
Eat and drink of Him constantly
Pray incessantly
Know that He is God, God of all, of everything

In Your Garments

Clothe me in Your garments
That I may feel Your presence
One of safety, one of love, Your gentle hug

Cover me with Your touch
Like magic dust
Sheltered completely, swaddled, wrapped

Clothe me, label me as Your own
So that I may reflect on my worth
My inner wool, my new birth

If I Lived a Thousand Times

If I lived a thousand times, each turn a hundred years
I would want to know my Lord
In different parts of the world, other years before
I bet each time
I would know Him more and more
I long for Him, this is my need

Is it sufficient, all this time that I should spend
That I could ever hope to understand
His magnitude, His grandeur, His everlastingness
Even if I asked for ten thousand more
Will I fully come to know
The Son of man

My time is His, Creator of night and day
It doesn't matter, the length of my stay
He planned it, my path determined and received
Who am I to contend
He shall reveal all to me in the end
As for now it is for me only to believe

Healing of a Broken Heart

It is amazing, it is great, that He alone can do this
In our suffering and our pain
In our cries for help and tears of sorrow
Believe Him and in Him, He has your tomorrow

It will pass, it always does, this broken heart
And He makes sure of this
The walk may be short or the journey long
He waits on you to join now that you have grown
See the foundation, the Rock, that stone

Oh Jesus, there You are, where have I been
I have been missing
Oh Jesus, I see now, more often than before
I have returned
Glory be to you God, for the rescue and restore

Fresh Start

Go on ahead, face the world
Go hard, start again bold
Feel no shame or embarrassment
Challenges are for growth and enrichment

If not the door, a window opens
In your best interest, it happens
You are ready now all rested and renewed
This is your time, a time for you

To do exciting things
Live and dream and laugh a lot
Leave all the baggage at the foot of the cross
Now that you know who is the real boss

Fresh start, fresh start here I come
Welcome me in your embracing arms
Have never been here before, I don't think
It is Your decree, this is for me, fresh start

Heaven on Earth

A glimmer of hope
A glimpse of nature
Could it be ....that heaven on earth

The birth of a new born babe
The birth too of a dream come true
Could it be.....that heaven on earth

An act of kindness and gentleness
A touch of love and happiness
Could it be....that heaven on earth

A friend with hands extended
A prodigal son's return and he is accepted
Could it be....

Holy Spirit Power

Visible in actions, heard in words
Felt in true love
Come Holy Spirit
Come

Inner truth, inner strength
Inner all
Come Holy Spirit
Come

Mistaken Identity

Sometimes I wish I were God and that I made you
That's how much I feel I love you

And I don't feel angry, just hurting for your hurting
That's how much my love hurts for you

If you would search for me then you would find me
One other wish

If you would knock then I would
open the door for you
Yet another too

I thought you were God and I know I am not He
Just believed you had that same kind of love for me

What I did not know then, was that it was not
But in fact a case of mistaken identity

I cannot be your God nor can you be my own
Blind before, now open wide are my eyes

Mistake mended, I understand like a bird
singing its song
In first place is where He alone belongs

The String around my Finger

Hello Father, I shall remember
Every part of me, Inch to iota
Created marvellously

See in my mirror, looking in deeper
The string around my finger
Like Father, like son

Your craft, your brand
Fashioned after You
Sincerely, Your lamb

Closed Eyes

I wonder how I would see him if I were blind
What I would look for and what I would find
Intangible treasures, blind I could see better
That's what I would see if I looked into his mind

I listen more carefully with closed eyes
No visual distraction
I pay attention to things that carry weight
The things that matter
Like honesty, integrity, love for humanity

I am more aware of my own feelings
They tell me, they warn me, they prepare me
So I shut my eyes, I search within the heart
I look into the mind for more
And I compare, to the only worthy standard
Of the One who loves me for sure

How Could I Forget

I say my prayers and a minute later
I forget about you
Here I go again, as if it is all about me
And I ignore that You are with me all day long
For years and years this was my song

Until that time when I was down and out
I thought not of me but You came to light
I said "Lord help me", You remember
And much more too
How can I forget that it's all about You

Yes, endless days and nights of weeping
Enduring I thought I could not
But here I am today
Alive and well and in love more with You
My Saviour and King, healing my brokenness too

I can no longer forget that it's all about you, Jesus
I am keeping you around, dear God
At the start and end My Lord
Throughout each day, please stay

Jesus is the Good News

Thank you for the Good News
The turning and affirming
Through baptism in Him
Forgiveness of sin
Through atonement by Him

This Great News You bring
From shadow to light, a new dawn
Life through the Son of man
My saviour, My Lord Jesus Christ
An invitation to all, outsiders, you belong

In a Basket

Bless the hands that placed me, secured me
Hello, it is I, little me, baby boy born to be
Later threatened and scorned, first loved and adorned
Saved, wrapped and floated away
Nursed by my own mother secretly
I shall set my people free one day, free a nation from slavery

Bless the hands that received me, saved me
Cuddled and cared for, like the son of a king
Envied and quietly dreaded by the blood son, born to him
Comforted in luxury, marinated in wealth
Any gift for me
Everything, yet I found empty

Bless the hands that fed me, clothed me
And when His hand was ready
And His cloak and robe I wore
He put His staff in my hand, this is really who I am
Instructed my way, I listened and obeyed
And Ten Commandments followed after that day

Bless the hands that guided me, led me
Led the chosen, no choice was Pharaoh given
He parted the Red Sea for me, for us to be free
Fed with manna
Our hope is in our God, a people still loved by the Father
My name is Moses, written destiny in a basket floated

His Grace is Sufficient

How very many stories have been heard
Of an emptiness transformed into fullness
In dire straits don't we enter, create
Improvise, abide new, ourselves dedicate

Like a new vessel, hands held up, ready to receive
And trusting because what is left is nothing
Knowing that what is coming must be better
Believing in a greater start for a different kind of
future

New clay in the potter's hands
More pliable, more willing, more doing
More everything, each moment in clinging
Now that emptiness performed disappearing

Filling to fulfil a path worth living
From suspension to flight
No more cocoon, like wings of a butterfly
Births another chance
With plenty enough from the Potter's hands

Explore With Him

It is always good to spread your wings
And explore
Look how many have done it before
Go fearlessly even if you are the first in your group
An excellent example for future troops

Some must lead and some must follow
Each with different gifts as He desires
Make it worth it bless the Lord
Whichever then should be your call

Whether you are following or leading
Remember to carry His compass
For directing and discerning
Spreading the word and exploring

Evergreen Spirit

The nature of trees
In changing seasons
Leaves us to believe
That change gives reason

Reason strong enough to move, to choose
Choose to have the ever spirit
Taking in all the worldly beauty around
And standing firm unmarred by it

No camouflaging, no chameleon
It is what it is, the Ever
Deep rooted, belonging, no bother
No colour changing, I'm not like the others
Shouting

What a spirit, what a faith
That a tree has been gifted with
How much more have we
Should we choose to receive it

I Shall Run to You

I shall run to you
Safe in your embrace
That in times of trials and distress
I shall run to You

Lord, surely You are ahead of me
Supplying all, restoring constantly
Why shall I not choose to be near to You
I shall run to you

At your side, in the shelter of Your wing
Clinging to You with my all, I bow
And against all things
Fearing nothing, I am with you now

Thoughts of Redemption

What would this look like
If I could touch, if I could feel
If I could paint a picture, so you could see
What it is to be redeemed

It's unequivocally, it's unconditionally
Love from above, His atonement
In spite of naughty, in spite of past,
present or future sin
His forgiveness before we were even sorry, a mystery

Not like some earthly vows
Yet like a ring in that it never ends
Through His word, through His promise
It's one of those things

No touch, no feel, His planning
Your knowing
And yes
To be redeemed is to believe

And if today, I were the worst sinner on the earth
I hope someone would tell me,
He died especially for me
Then I would have these thoughts of redemption
I would choose to say yes to His invitation,
to salvation

JO ANNE C. BLACKMAN

This Peace

Pursue peace
And realize your smile
While changing seasons
It's heaven on earth, in all weather
Yours to guard and treasure

Given for your happiness
Yours for the keeping, amazing
And even in that moment undiscerning
When your thoughts want to stray
Still you possess it, an anchor it stays

From baby crawls to toddler steps
A mature spirit accepts it
With faith and trust, this peace, it lasts
Captivated
In your sincere heart it resides at last

Let Me

That you must seek me
So I can help you find your way
What kind of riddle must I be

Or, is it simply
Because you're prone to go astray
You need to turn my way

Then take my Word as your own
And walk where I show
The Light you need to know

Give me the key to turn your heart
Let me revise your path
Revive your soul, let me make you whole

JO ANNE C. BLACKMAN

Close to You Lord

I pray this prayer to you Father
Keep me close to you Lord
My hands are clasped together
Keep me close to you Lord
My eyes are closed, I am on my knees
Keep me close to you Lord
And solemn, my head bowed down
Keep me close to you Lord
Amen

Keep Your Eyes on Me

Do not look away least you stray
Stay with me, my child, walk with me, pray
For I am always with you
I love you

Put no other first, this is the only way
To live in light and truth each day
For I am always with you
I love you

Challenges you will have, sure you may fall
Look to me first, I will lift you up, I will answer your
call
For I am always with you
I love you

Oh good soil you have my seed, take firm root in me
Anchor yourself to grow strong and resemble me
For you are My own, you are like me, I love you
Says the Lord

The Prize Inside
(Oyster, Egg and the Human-kind)

Pretentious and bold
Wicked and twisted, he knows the worth of inside
The true treasure of the world, your soul

As with an oyster
The shell is useful to some certainly
Then further in, fleshy, tempting and tasty
But at the heart, if time you wait
Lies it's pearl, the inner beauty

Now with the egg, the shell you remember
Humpty-Dumpty in rhyme and play
Then other players, more than the membrane
There after lay, the yoke, the inner core
Yellow and white, the part we all hope for

And you and I, created in so much more detail
Our body is our shell, intricately designed
To pleasure the eyes and still guarding inside
But when we lose to flesh, arrives
The one who thinks he is wiser than wise

It is no secret, that liar, he roams and he lies
And to the unsuspecting
Awaits that slip, that slide, to snatch
With a brash move or consistently subtle
His desperate goal, to devour the prized prize

Look to the Cross

It's not that we don't know or that we don't care
But the fact that we don't say no
That threatens our soul
The forces about, roam as they may
For one reason, day by day, to pull us away

And true it is a struggle for us all
Sometimes we stand firm and a lot of times, fall
And true, we all are weak
But where do we look for strength to defeat

On our own it is impossible
Together with Him, the opposite occur
Take up your cross, battle to the end
Send an alarm, say "Lord please Help"

It's never too late to start afresh
That's why Jesus died, sacrificed in flesh
Repent, and sin no more
That is His message
Not about settling a score

JO ANNE C. BLACKMAN

Mercy and Grace

Mercy to carry me when I am too weak
Not that I am deserving but that I am loved
And grace to take me forth in perfect timing
In perfect charge
Like a full strong wind, directing
Yet blowing from a gentle giant's mouth

Together they strengthen my moves, my path
All encompassing, not forgetting my past
Leading me into a future at last
Mercy and grace that I should have
Outlining me, lining my heart
Receiving them both, a wonderful start

I First Pictured You

You are my sheep, my own
I see all your days, I hear all your crying out
Do not be afraid
Trust in me, trust in my ways
Come to me, as when
You first walked
Growing out of your crawl
And I caught you before the fall
Turn to me, as when
I first pictured you
Let me, complete the wonder in you
One that is true
Trust in me, as when
I first pictured you

Pray for All

Doesn't every one of us need prayer
Who should be denied, or who should deny this
Its helpfulness, its necessity, its cure
Pray then for me

Who should be denied, or who should deny this
A prayer for those, not wanted, rejected
The nothing leaving them empty inside
Pray still for them

Its helpfulness, its necessity, its cure
The receiving leaves you wanting more
A filling, of the unseen pit that lies forgotten
Pray always, it is written

No Mirage

Who is this
My oasis in the dessert
No mirage
The one who cares

Who is this
My fearless in the midst of fear
Knight of nights
The one who cares

Who is this
My true beacon, light
Morning star
The one who cares

Who is this
My peacemaker in storms
Touching, bringing calm
Inner, physical, all

He is my God

Perfect Love

The greatest love
You can ever have
Is the love
Freely given from above

It's the happiness you seek
That lives in giving
As He gave His life
To bring us to our everlasting

No other love
Can begin to compare
To His perfect love
For you everywhere

Servant of the Lord

I am a servant of the Lord
I want to be obedient, but not all the time I can
I want to love Him the way He loves me, Impossible
I pray fervently for His wisdom in me

This here servant of the Lord
Has refused to take along heavy loads, burdens
He spoke to me, He told me, let them to me
Only when I listened to His voice I heard

Humble servant of the Lord I remain
Forever representing Him
In my thoughts, words and deeds
Only with Him, shall I even try to succeed

I Say You Are

I say you are love, my God
My saviour, God incarnate, my Lord
My hope, joy, happiness all
That's who I say You are

I say you are my brother, sister
My husband, wife, friend
My before, now and end
That's who I say You are

I say you are the way, the truth and the life
Creator all-knowing and wise
Glorious, magnificent, Holy mystery
That's who I say You are

I say you are my eat, my drink
My teacher and inner strength
Son of God, the Messiah
That's who I say You are

I say you are gentle and loving
Giving and all sacrificing
You are my peace
That's who I say You are

I say you are goodness in mankind
Hope for mankind at the end of time
My never ending rhyme
That's who I say You are

Saying Glory to You Lord

I have been blessed with a surge of comforting words
It's not me, Glory to you Lord
Never knew I had it in me, a late bloomer I must be
Still it's not me, Glory to you Lord

A dear friend of my rhymes said, "What fine lines"
I was quick to reply, without delay
It is the Word most definitely
Not me, Glory to you Lord

"Don't waste your new talent", she then explained
"None will be wasted", I replied, "it is for a gain"
To spread His joy, His hope, the Word
Throughout the world, Glory to you Lord

Your BFF

Greater love, none but His
Tell Him, tell Jesus
His will, His answer
His perfect timing forever

Keep Him closer than any other
Your *Best Friend Forever*
Resist the detour
Forgiveness personified
Provision for life when He died

With a contrite heart, a humble soul
You are after all, His own
Like a dove taking flight
Up goes your prayer, everyone He hears
Be still now in secret fasting, wait
And know His purpose for you, is one great

Where are You Love

Massage my shoulders, rub my back
Hold my hands, with me walk
Where are you love

Meals I create for us to share
Some 9-5 for me, my real work is Poetry
Where are you love

In my leisure, picture painting I will do
My past time is being with you
Where are you love

Oh, that I would make that mistake repeat
To live absorbed in you, then I forfeit
Where are you love

If I really looked and found the you
The you, the one I need to know
Then would I say, here You are, Lord

Transformation

Thank you for starting the good work in me
Opening my blind eyes, my deaf ears
Sealing my lips like... like biting my tongue
So I can just be
Reminding me of your presence and awesomeness
Your magnificence and without You
My insignificance

Thank you for opening Your door
For taking me on long walks so I can ponder
About Thee
Hand in hand, eyes through eyes, on my knees
Forgetting of myself,
instead thinking of Your thoughts
As You speak, knowing me
Knowing my thoughts

Thank you that You are, the great I AM
Above all creation
Looking down on me as I lay or stand
Loving me, wanting me, pursuing me
And transforming me
That I may walk in gratitude and humility
O Sacred Heart, more like you shall I be

Looking Up What Do I See

Lying on my bed
Through the window the clouds take form
My imagination makes them what I want
They twist and twirl into something beautiful
My eyes see what they want to see

Blue sky, they travel on like the sea
May as well be, for they seem to blow to and fro
Like a sailboat with the waves and the wind
Or an archer pulling his bow and arrow

And further in the corner as far as I can see
Though I know no corner can there be
I captured a magnificent sight, look now
You can see it too, look it is true

It's the hand of the artist, the author, our Creator
I looked some more trying to find
The rest of Him to no avail
Then I looked about to realize He is everywhere
Right here...do you see

Rock Standing

Because He loves me
Because it's all about Him
I must remember
I can always tell Him

Anything and everything
Through every season, through every land
He is my all, the One
The rock on which I stand

Reaching Through

Praise the Lord and give Him glory
As if to touch the sky
And reaching for His hands
Plug into Him, stretch long and tall
Closing your eyes
Now reaching through the sky

Never mind if you falter
We are His, He already knows
Try, you must reach again and again
If you slip, your right hand He shall take
And lift you right up again

Compassionate
And full of grace
Is our Lord of love and tenderness
Recall the cross, the risen One
Recall the promise attached to it
Detaching sin through Him
Believe now and reach...... for Him

You Lord...my everything

Jesus, my king, my friend and my brother
Be my everything in this world as the other
Help me to be dedicated to serving You
Teach me Your ways and allow me to change
From old to new

Set my heart on fire with Your love
Let peace set in like Your most Holy Dove
Take my broken self, my thoughts
Words and actions, my all
Mold me for Your purpose, to answer your call

Every day where ever I am, where ever I go
With every one, whoever they are
Whomever they know
It will matter not, Your will be done
Whatever your plan for me, let it be

So my Lord and Saviour, be my everything
You know my cry, my everything
Heal me, strengthen me, guide me and protect me
From all that is not of You in this world
With your blood cover me

I Found My Comforter True

Seek and you shall find
I found my comforter true
In loving kindness came you
The awakening of my baptism

Mistakes I made before
Looking where no solace lay
My search was in vain
Stay did my pain until all I gave Him

To stand with Him through each day
My burdens have gone away
He carries them for me as He promised
He handles me, places me where I should be

And now no sorrow do I hold, no sadness do I keep
My true comfort is He
My heart is held in His, my soul is His
I am so glad I found Him, my own

In Solitude

In a space where no one, none can touch me
But yet He alone
Reaches

In meditation I stay for as long as I wish
And it is here
He blesses

In the silence where here he talks and teaches
So I can hear His voice
And listen

It is where I am now, to quiet my soul
And rest in His presence
Cradled in His palm and hushed by His eyes
In solitude

Your Gift

From Your Spirit my gift has been endowed
One long hidden
For I cannot explain how
How I came to be doing all of this writing now

So totally grateful I am to be blessed in this way
It gives me joy and happiness
To be able to serve today
To share of the Word, Your love each day

This is my offering, some to go and some to stay
First to help the Word go far
And then to some more poor
After which, I will use the rest to build up
My words restore

Letter to the Lord...
Dearest Father

Most of all for your presence in my life every day
For loving me in my imperfection
Thank you Lord anyway
For the blessing of wonderful God fearing parents
Who raised me in love and tenderness
So that I may come to know
You Father as loving and tender

For the blessing of my brothers and sisters
My spouse and children, my grandson
Nieces and nephews
God children and for the dear friends
Whom you have placed in my life
For angelic strangers who serve your purpose

For all that you have given and taken
All that you have shown and hidden
For the joys and sorrows, for your wisdom
And loving kindness
Mercy and grace, the fruits of your Holy Spirit
For a future with you today and tomorrow
Your promises, thank You for everything

Yours, JC

Section Two

Encouragement Galore

Dear Friends

Especially chosen, just for me
Though I do not see you every day, it wouldn't matter
Know for sure your friendship is real for me
as it is for you
You are deep in my heart, for what we share is truth

We are friends in Christ,
what better could there ever be
Brothers and sisters in the faith
that our Redeemer lives
So the love we share, is the love He gave
How fortunate are we, to have His saving grace

You are strong as you are compassionate
Enduring this life, in the greater hope of salvation
I see grace and kindness in your faces
And from your mouths, thanks and praise

So, thank you
In your perfect imperfection
In being human
Dear friends, I love you

Such Haste

Why do I write in such haste
Words set in my mind, just waiting to arrive
As if I had to write what I write
Least the time like vapour, passes bye

In the nights, when I have retired
Still busy are my thoughts
Of first nothing, at once then everything
I quickly render pen and paper writing

To capture that seemingly infinite moment
When such profound meaning comes to mind
Still I do not understand
This haste which I have found

For a purpose, it must be
An awakened breeze
Blowing and bursting through me
The Spirit of God shining and alive in me
I AM, He hastens, for it is He

Saucy Mammy
(Mommy Dearest, we all love you)

Hello Madam, how are you
Madam, what are you up to
You know, you are quite a source
To think about and draw from, of course

And I am one of some, many if lucky
Privileged to share, the juice
Madam Dear, thank you
Hello, hear me now, you are Mommy

I am jokingly stating, though most seriously
Madam, Mommy, Saucy Mammy too
The advice you give from knowing God
Is yet another gift wrapped in you

Through My Eyes

Since you were a babe, even after every time
You always seemed and knew
Exactly what you wanted too
I quite like and admire that strong spine
I should learn from your climb

All the while so tenderly loving
Soft and under a shell guarding
A heart of gold, purest silver
Or a precious metal undiscovered
My darling beautiful sibling

You can mommy me too
I see how you both, with your jewel do
I know you have taught her to care
And so grateful that makes me, of you we can share
Never ever shall there be rivalry

Human Super Hero

Sounds like my Dad, with a cape
My Dad, my hero, handling all with grace
Having to live up to expectations
Maybe of others, but I think by choice, his own
Humbly heroic

With a face handsomely chiseled
And a body developed to match
A physique that mirrored Clark Kent's, or Captain
American's
And a kind and gentle heart
Having then, to put up moral boundaries
To protect the integrity of his family
My treasured memories

His hobbies kept him keenly occupied
And his humour for which to die
Never letting you down on his promises
It was always thought through, a home run
Of my recollection, never a miss

JO ANNE C. BLACKMAN

I imagine, he must have had great challenges
Now that I am much older, in somewhat his position
Glad to know that his passions, he was able to share
With someone beautiful, to him invaluable
Invaluable still

The invisible hero, quietly behind the scene
Would be his confidant, close companion, spouse
My Mom, encouraging and supporting him all along
So all in all they were the Incredible Dual, two in
one...
My parents

Both for Me

Both for me, but different completely
Treasured, none the less
Thank you bros, over the years
Your kindness and understanding
Even with each other is something

Something that not everyone shares
And in very tiny ways, it is evident
That love and compassion is alive
And the desire to strive, is lent
One to the other as time goes by

Looking in my mind, picture finding
Many great times of laughing
And thinking of the now and after
I have decided
I am keeping you both, my brothers

Losing You

How selfish of me to carry on this way
Why does this grief hang on and stay
What don't I understand, after so long
That I well up so often, tearing and torn

Such fantastic memories, a true blessing for me
It's not that I'm ungrateful
I suspect some selfishness
To have to give you back so fast, impossible to see
I had imagined at least double your time
Here with me

One may think you were my spouse or even baby
But in fact you were my Daddy, dear Daddy
I miss you so, even though for sure I know
We will meet again, in that perfect place
The Golden space

Clergy & Company

This company was Holy, reminding me of Him
A flock of sheep,
Now shepherds, after His own heart
Many hands, His

With an immediate welcome
Not a stand offish beaconing in
But a warm and sincere treatment
For a wounded lamb, just needing

And prayers offered for my distress
With wisdom and clarity
Of what is most important
The Father's love for me

Thank you Clergy and Company
You too are in my prayer
That many, many more lambs you shall tend
And blessings from the Father, never shall they end

Please, Madam
("I don't have a topic, don't force me")

I wish to write of your topic
Madam, would you please
Think of one, give me your pick
It would mean a lot to me

To which was your reply
Don't have one, my dear
And don't appreciate the pressure
Stop if you care

Madam, it is not what it seems
For care I do indeed
This is why, for you I wish to write
Some beautiful poetry

Birth of a Dream

Wanted from the start, in the earlies
Last of my three cuties
Late winter, before spring
That's when you came into being

Cutie Patootie, that was you
Perfect attention given then
By that time I was a pro
And you made it easy, all 12 inches head to toe

And growing slowly, up you came
Through those trying teenage pains
So what, everyone makes a mistake and some
I believe you have learned, that time is all gone

Persevere, press on and press on
And for your dreams to come through
I told you the secret true, keep the faith
Make sure you do

JO ANNE C. BLACKMAN

Did You Know

Intense thoughts, you seem to hold
So funny, to hear you laugh alone

Observing, you seem to be somehow engaged
Your listening not to be disparaged

Creative in music, words and beats for long
And the writing of many songs

Serious when it comes to your dollar
Definitely with you, no messing fella

When you are relaxed and around
Better everyone prepare to have fun

Your eyes connect in piercing form
Like when you touch, it reaches the storm

Eating, you enjoy and from a long while back
Back when you were a tot, neither was there lack

When not even one, fussing for baby brew
Then milk was done, out from the crib the bottle flew

Different sports a natural at, not much effort
Like a foot fits a shoe, that's you

Encouragement Galore

You are something else, one of a kind
Kind still you are and value you lend
Opinions worth counting, and counting on I can
A gracious blend

You are my friend, new though you are
New to me, but wise indeed
I find sincere, wouldn't trade you in
I cherish your advice and follow your lead

You know it's now, these found words I adore
Can't seem to get them out of my mind
But I am glad, thank God, they are a find
Like you, encouragement galore

Entrusted

I have known her all her life
I reflect and sometimes, I cry
Buckets a drop, so much
When I recall past joys
I am sentimental, like that

Dear to me, I call her Neenee
She's gorgeous, quite the entertainer too
And beautiful right through
Another nick name, Ruthee, my one and only
I love nicknames, she's Daughtee

No, no I do not boast of her
But of the Creator, and thankful for
This borrowed gift of delight
I couldn't ask for better
I believe, none other would suffice

One of my little loves, entrusted
And should you have one lent to you
To safeguard and raise up
Then you must know of what I speak
True, whether girl or boy for you

Saying Goodbye

I know I'll see you again, it's only before noon
But I feel so uncertain about
when you'll be coming back
Although every day you always do
I am trapped in the loss of someone very dear
Many years aback

So it's with that in mind, that my mind plays
A deep horrid feeling of something grand being lost
And when I look as you go off, it's with a prayer
That I'll see you soon again my dear

If I seem sad as you depart, and you spot a little tear
It's not at all unhappiness, but again that awful fear
I'd love to put it to rest, but it latches on to my heart
When I begin to think of losing another
and having to part

I hope one day I would come to terms
And instead wave and laugh as you drive off
Knowing for certain that it is not goodbye
But ... love you, see you, no one else's but mine

JO ANNE C. BLACKMAN

Strength Grace and a Lot Wise

Wisdom, countenance straight, that's you
And when laughter slips one in
You can bet it's a good one too

Laughter, laughter come along
Like the time on the train
Uncontrollable and rolling, giggling and some
Mouths stretched from ear to ear
Cheeks plump to pinch, eyes watering our chins
Good genes, good genes

Was dat ting, an fur dis an dat
Member den
My long time fren
That lickle book from the West Indian store
Too funny the words, funnier each time more
Another day like that, I'd gladly attend

Right now, before long gone is after
I want to say, how much I admire
Your style of strength, grace and wisdom

Papa and Me

When Papa comes in, I hear the door
I get so excited as he comes up the stairs
My eyes lock to his
And we give a nod, as he stops his walk
That's how we talk

When I say "Hi Papa" he is in shock
Not knowing what to say, he still nods
I wonder about this Papa, what are his thoughts
When will he talk

He plays with me in different ways, almost to tease
I learn so quickly
He is amazed, it's instant replay, that's me
We must be related Papa, can't you see

Did you know, when you fall sound asleep
I touch you and poke you
Try to open your eyes too
Papa, I am learning about love, loving you

A Face to Look at

To stare at your eyes
Innocence and peace
Tiny little nose
And a mouth sleeping closed

Even though you sleep
Your brows move up and down
Mouth smiling now
Under your new chin
Tiny, tiny hands propping

As if thinking
To play and dance and sing
To live and love and laugh
No wonder, I am gazing

It Was He

Your fortitude through the travel
If you were to be asked
Always remains the same
It's not me......it was He

Then more travel as it were
How was it done, I would replay
Constant as you stay
Your reply, not surprising....it was He

In astonishment of your road so far
One of my own, I could not imagine
Again, same words repeating
In your calm confidence....it was He

And still my exemplar
Imperfect to others maybe, but a saint to me
How much more can you ask of a Mommy
Thank you Mommy, for telling me.....it was He

Inspiration

That God would use you to inspire me
For you talk of Him with grand adoration
As if love was a parcel, real to touch and feel
I mean, rather vividly revealed

Your words are full, like a blossoming flower
Picturesque, a garden where He tends
And we praised Him, it must have been plus an hour
Recollecting His absolute supremacy and power

When you can talk freely about our Daddy
His Holy Spirit is hovering gladly
And about the greatest sacrifice ever
Believing, even though in parcel, you met Him never

You are answering courageously
Your work is surely His calling
There can be no denying, He is love
Keep on inspiring, He is the King

Ordinary People Extraordinary Folks

I listened to some ordinary people
I really did
As they wished if they could wish
Things I could never believe
Like world peace

Things I didn't wish for
Thinking impossible
Like to be forgiven
And to give others forgiveness

I look back now in admiration
Of these extra-ordinary folks
Who dared to wish and to believe
It was their faith, their hope

Their thoughts must have been so pure
Imagining a heaven here on earth
Bless them and may they, in numbers grow
And their wishes endure

JO ANNE C. BLACKMAN

Swinging Again

Swinging in the front yard
Sweet children play
Sharing happy songs, of a friend's party day
The forming of an unknown friendship
to be discovered some day

And there they were again
Never knowing their paths would intertwine
Hugging and talking, destined
As if it were yesterday
all caught up, in a single smile

Everyone should have one
A sister, a brother, a best friend
You would think my clone
For me, it's like having the hand
of God lent, like swinging again

Hello Small Group
(Imagine...many small groups)

That creation can constantly be renewing
With deep contemplation of the crucifixion
Drawing from the source of source
In full communion with God by praying

Communion with God, in heavy doses
Neither dribbling nor sprinkling
Learning the Word, reading bible verses
Not religious, rather decided soaking

Helping those days of dismal
To the table, hope and light bringing
Prayers in agreement, the Small Group sharing
Coming together, supporting one another

Like a symphony playing, much to His pleasure
Concerted and dedicated sharing of the One
Feeding from the Source, the true Vine
From the time, our Small Group began

In Good Time Good Friend

You came around, just before
As if placed, for a time ahead
A knitted fit for me, you when
Into the 9-5 arrived

You seemed to discover in me
A dire need for company
And then you arranged
As you always do, a plan to bring relief

Through the years, always there
Unscheduled, but as often as we needed
You popped in, you stopped the bleeding
Thank you sunshine, you are a beam

Just a Little Naughty

If I didn't know any better
I would say that you are His follower
Telling me about not believing in The Higher Power
How then is it, that you are such a great imitator

And your outlook is so thankful
As you are and always were beautiful
Kind and considerate, funny too and just a little
naughty
Some would now say, a strong personality

Made exactly as he decided
With his hands moulded
And all of His creation He loves
In our hearts, He gave His holy dove

I want to say that I love you...so "I love you"
And I give God all the glory
For making you so perfectly friendly
Making you, a friend for me

Lines Passed On

Thank you, for the most gracious compliment
On my seemingly solid form
From friend to friend and passed on
Oh, how I would like it to go on
Only if more time spared some

It feels grand to hear
These wonderful cheering words
Not flattered though
Rather most humbly, I
Accept your kind lines

Please relay to our friend
Still where from, this form comes
Although you see me
It is on the Rock I stand
He is the One, holding my form

My Dear Honey...

With that smile you wore, I looked for, while I waited
Where at the stop we first met
Impossible, never to forget...you
And Monday to Friday I hoped to meet
Again and again, didn't want it to end
Kind words shared, of family time

Upon your head a wig covering
Knew not at all, that you were ailing
May be it was because, we were always laughing
Years gone by, one day at the train, couldn't
recognize
Thought I saw you standing, you had grown thin
You called me out, before then we were closer
friends

Movie going, the one with Oprah and Danny Glover
I know you didn't like to drive, me neither
I never told you, just came and got you, I was your
driver
You made a joke about his dusty feet
And wished he was casted for a different part
We did observe and laugh, that Beloved
We never understood it
Strange, we remarked

JO ANNE C. BLACKMAN

You invited me, I brought the little ones too
And we had an evening of cake, tea and lovely
company
Excited, swiftly moving to the back
Bursting through your screen door
I remember your yard, in the corner
Beautiful orange flowers, Lilies, that time I came over
And when you dropped by my place, for lunch, Corn-
Pie
Anxious to taste the dish and eat
You exclaimed, "Where is the meat"

Our little sons played together,
Up to now they glimpse each other
Vinnie and Chris now a score plus more
And your daughter Shelley to my Ruthee was some
older
But I remember thinking, what a role model
Your Chad was in the middle, a bit shy
And my Tike, you adored him, the baby of the pile

Even though that difficult stuff, caused us to drift
You went out of your way, for me you stayed
When I think of you, your big smile comes to mind
And if I continue, my smile I shall find
Your hubby and you, both kind to me
Your very loving family
I'll never forget you, my dear honey

I know He has you in His hands, away from all pain
And suffering
You be good for now, and one day then
We shall be laughing again
I want to say love you to death, but we know it is
now life
Life through Christ, Life in Christ, your life
Everlasting life, Honey Dear

Sister Lovely

How shall I begin, to start and state
That without doubt or fail
You are incredibly great

A gentle kindness that in friends you find
How lucky I am that you are mine
Special to many I'm certain

Certainly if I had a choice to pick
I would call you sister
Sister you are in any case

Lovely comes front of mind
When I recall our many times
Caring and hearing me plenty

And plenty more times I wish we can share
So my care I may also express
To someone I hold in high regard...my sister lovely

The Lord's Helper

He came unexpectedly, into my world
Joy and play and wonderful this tiny one
He is my first grand, my grandson

So unique, I mean of my own I have three
But this little fellow is exciting and new
He is Isaiah, the Lord's helper too

A sound sleeper from early on
Smiling as he tries to say Good Morning
Walking and running some falling

He is a true thinker, even long before
He was singing Bless the Lord My Soul
10 000 reasons to love him more

Oh little one, so precious
This joy you bring is blessed
Yes, the Lord's helper, the meaning of-Isaiah

From Time Before

Solemn was your face when I first saw you
A special kind of quiet drew me near you
No fuss but deep engrained purpose
Ploughing through our moments
Soil and grain tilling, but for us, not toiling

A sense to care, like a mirror, a twin
For each other, time well spent
And even though it seems a late start
We are so far ahead, to an abounding path

Then continue on we must this quest
To learn from each other relentlessly
His love so great it is the power
He is our Pillar, the awesome Tower

Time in His hands is just a trickle
Designed by Him a tiny sprinkle
Seems that I have always known you
From time before, I then saw you

So Softly Able

It's true, that's you
Too fond of you, I am, you must know
When I needed your care
Kind hearted, so softly able you were

If only for the lending of your ear, was all
Not true, but your natural ability to be, so sensible
Truly considerate and
So softly able

Including me in endless walking
Dear you, thanks for bearing me through
And that time of weekly mind stretching
So softly able, good hearted that's you

The Story Found in You

A breath of fresh air, and elegance tall
A mind so bright and sharp and quick
Quick as the light, that fills your face
Hello Gorgeous, hello beautiful

A pleasant personality, is an understatement for me
It's that stand, that glow
No one could know, from that instant
No one would bet, yet

With eyes that tell and search at once
They pierce gently and connect the common
A story of hope and trust and awesomeness
The story found in you, in your courage and kindness

Many would never dare, but I get you
You take the chance because you care
Hello Gorgeous, you say
And for no other reason but, how was your day

My Childlike Heart

I know you know, from a whisper before
I love you mommy, I love you more
More than yesterday, each day
Growing because you are, simply you.... mom

It should be easy for me, to express most eloquently
But for words, would you believe
Frozen are my thoughts and at a loss
Maybe better expressed, instead
With my eyes, staring up adoring you

Or better yet, my tummy warms as if hugged
In anticipation of your demonstrated love
And my childlike heart, it jumps, it bounces about
From a whisper to a shout out
Still I love you more

JO ANNE C. BLACKMAN

People in Your Life

They help and influence and shape eventually
A seed, planted so purposefully
The soil of which hopefully, rich
That roots took firm hold, supporting upward bliss

Fathers, mothers, brothers, sisters
For a start, the family, an important part
And extended to the Grands and cousins too
The making of a you

The teachers, whether friends, aunties or uncles
Educators and religious, entertainers and others
The community, social media, internet
Much for us to digest, world now at our fingertips

Back to your Vine, the heart of your stand
Through all the seasons, they clung on
Being branches for strength to each draw on
Heart of your stand, true relationship with God,
the One

Purposeful Rescue

A thought that overwhelms
Worries that weigh you to bend
I can never say I understand
For our storms, are not the same
But in your eyes, I see your pain
Reminding me once of my own

I shudder to think
I shiver to know
What can you be going through
That makes your weeping
Sweeping, to drown out the happy in you
It reminds me of me
Before I knew what to do

I can say with certainty
That there is one who truly loves you
Hard to receive, this good news
But I am here to tell you
It is the truth
Believe, all things are possible
Our God is here to rescue you

Until Next Time

A walk and a laugh to over there
Before then came, Hello
So good to see you
Now catching up for a year

A brilliant choice to lay back, relax
With an hour or two to spare
A retreat with new colours for our fingers and toes
Pampering our hands and our feet

Come noon, good company continuing
Good food and dessert following
Did we sip wine
And was that one day in August enough time

But it's Good Bye for now
Never ever sad, just until
A hand or call, a text or email
Until next time

Section Three

Hope

Just My Thoughts

In my sharing I wish you to relate
To plant yourselves in my words and rhymes
Deep into just my thoughts partake

Still to create a nudge, a stir, some reflect
To enjoy or converse or react
To think and rethink and act

My real editors are you
From all cross sections you possess for sure
Mixed life experiences galore

As with you, never exchanging your past so precious
And me in bending and breaking now mending new
My experiences are my treasures too

Be good with you, your best friend in loving and
living
Believing in believing true therapy
These are my thoughts, given in poetry

Flying Pigs

Pigs are flying all the time
It's all in your mind
Not that you are losing it
But rather trying to keep it

Pigs are flying all the time
It's what you can look forward to
It happens without reason or rhyme
Just not all in your time

Pigs are flying all the time
You individually play a big part, if too they fly
It's the hope in store for your climb
Fly pigs fly, fly pigs fly

99 Plus 1 & Counting

By 5's and 10's each day came new tidings
One over the other so soon piling
#5, I recall, not completed yet
But thoughts of numbers 6 to 9
Gaining strong, before their time

Suddenly with the blink of my eye
My list was at forty-six
Thinking then, stop at 50 I shall soar
But much to my delight and awe
Faster was I with much more

They came into fruition, they came
And lo, ipso- facto, that day the big 50
Then by the 10's daily
So quickly came numero 90
I imagined a new goal, a game

Grand Finale may as well be 99 plus 1
That was my plan
A dear friend said to me
OMG...this is more than a roll
And you know what, she was right
This poetry was all about Him
Strengthening me

JO ANNE C. BLACKMAN

Anchor

Where can I find my anchor
I search for one with no success
You may ask, why then do I not find
My anchor that I may rest

I say I search, but really I do not
I suspect that is the reason
For the anchor still I lack
Maybe, this is not for me

You see I cannot seem to agree
This anchor, they say I should have
Perhaps I am not ready for
A gift, I feel undeserving of

When I am ready to settle down
Then my search will slow
I expect an anchor will find me
In spite of past, the drifting shall no longer be

To stay me and hold me
Keep me stable in my place
That I may acquire, rest finally
My anchor for me

Backbone

From your heart, speaks the strength of the bone
And your tongue rolls it out, with convincing tone
If you have a back bone

Everyday choices to make, in every interaction
Will it be a yes or a no
Ask your backbone

Difficult times need a backbone shout
Mustered up courage
Backbone kind of stuff, no bluff

And those unexpected challenges
How does the backbone address it
With crippling and curling or straight, tall standing

Soul food, some of that mysterious thing
Strengthening your everything
Always works for your invisible spine

Hold That Water In Your Mouth

Giddy- up giddy- up, off you go
Hold your tongue, don't you know
Silence is golden

No gossip and no idle talk at last
If time to spare in private pray and fast
Silence is golden

That itchy mouth, bursting with vocabulary
Will make your life burdensome and weary
Silence is golden

Hush now, except for words true
Let no lie be told from you
Silence is golden

Hold that water in your mouth
Be still and know that I am God
Silence is golden

Bottled Neck

Thoughts coming and going, ruining a flow
Unsettled, busy, then bottled neck to halt
You want to speed, He needs you to slow
To grab your attention, a sign He shows

He clears the way, the debris He removes
And in your waiting, like in fasting
You learn to yearn
To recognize Him

In your lane, strength entering
Because you needed Him
Your slow no longer grows, now you step again
You learn, your halt a passing thing

As He Levels the ground, so you can see
The peril you were in
Now every day, you walk with Him
"To be bottled neck is not a bad thing"
...it's what you now think

Oh Simple Joy

Through the white frame of my back door
Blinds drawn apart
Like a picture
Great blue sky at the top
And a line of Evergreens, descends from tall to dot
Borders the right

Left, some changing from green to maroon
Blinding the bricks next door
Those vines creeping up, with colours more
Now I gaze
At the base, the turning of my greenish grass
Another year, another chance
Fall on us new season, new song, new dance

Oh simply joy, I can see and enjoy
Observing the spin, this time round
Embracing creation, this new season
Frees my mind to think
My eyes to roam at least a thousand blinks
The ones, I missed the year before

Sitting, my feet as if blinking too
Unconsciously tapping a rhythmic bounce
Tap-tap, tap-tap....
As though enveloped themselves
In a beautiful trance
Enjoying this moment before it's done
Fall on us new season, new song, new dance

Go, Beacon, Go

As a beacon, my light flickers too
For strong winds bellow and blow me through
Trying to shut me up and shut me down
My shine is my sound

If I had a voice, but oh yes I do
A voice that eyes could see
I would shout so hard, some would blink
Every time they look at me

Happy then for those seeking me
Like an answer to a question
No longer strangers, they see me clearly
They steer closer, they draw nearer and nearer to me

Heading Home

It is for rest, I search desperately
I long to see the jetty
Shelter from drifting constantly
I can live no more with this pulling and tugging
Where to, shall I really be heading

On that day I will rejoice
When exile throws me back, heeding my voice
And my pleading is heard, I shall be in
When worry gives me up, no thoughts toil
And my feet hits the jetty first, then the soil

To make use of the force here or stay and be
The force to push me, no more sea
Into where a tree I may peep
Yes the tree, land is near

And finally "a jetty"...I exclaim
Lost, beaten and washed to shore
Forgotten is that sea, no more, no more
I am ready for a change

Hurry up, Heart

Hurry up heart you are lagging behind
For I have already made up my mind
My mind is wise and knows
My heart still acting slowly

Hurry up heart why wait
Your hurt seems so great
Unbearable for the mind to bear
Because of your surviving I care

Hurry up heart can't you see
This change you seek is not of me
Another heart another mind
There this change shall you find

Hurry up heart follow me
Come on, even piggy back on me
To where you are deserved and deserving
Treasured in whole, heart to soul, true loving

JO ANNE C. BLACKMAN

Hope

Oh hope, where are you, have you disappeared
If only you were here, then I could really dream
For I wish I could, but no.... I can't, you are gone
And I am stuck, not knowing what to do
Swallowed in a storm

Oh hope, have I forever lost you
or misplaced you only
Shall I search, without you I am lonely
What shall I do, where will I turn
Search for me hope, help me find you
Let your hand find my own

Oh hope, you found me, at last now I know
Never to separate from you, I shall never let you go
You are my breath
Keeping me alive and yearning for more
Stretching out to me

You hope, you believe in me
In years to come, I shall look back and see
That it was because of you, I am here
Living my life, in you............
Hope, you came for me

Smile Again

The stern of black and white
Softened with the colour of your smile
A canvas now showcasing
A different kind of style
Smile again beautiful, smile

Emotions held in tight as a fist
Only intended to resist
Not wanting to risk
Then the corners of your mouth motions up
Out shouts your smile
A breakthrough
Smile again beautiful, smile

The days found in February's leap
The world stops when you smile
As if to glimpse this moment finding
For it knows only for a while
Smile again beautiful, smile

JO ANNE C. BLACKMAN

If Wishes were Horses

Mice would be scientists
The inventors of cures
Better still no illnesses
We never die, no tears in our eyes
Dogs would be our masters, they wish
We would fetch them papers
They taught us tricks
Taxi drivers would be in charge
Of all traffic light signals, oh dear
Real home cooked meals would appear
With eyes winking
No chores, no dishwasher
No wares in the sink
And babies would be born
Doing their own changing
Wouldn't that be something, a dream

Work, we would love
Like our favourite game
Not a drag a lift
Bosses would even insist
That we work less when sick, a rare
And our pay, incentives
Bonuses would automatically be more
No anger would exist, no war
No famine, no greed
Mankind without iniquities
One God the only truth not if wished
But indeed for all to believe, our gift
Beggars don't ride, but God our Father
He lives forever, He is alive

My Mindset

How could I have thought that I was any better
Better off it would appear, but in no way better, true
Maybe I sounded better, but really to whom
Does is even matter, what is the fuss all about
About who is better than whom

Apparel fine, head held up high
Transportation is new, a sight for the eyes
Deep down I wish I were you, so different and sure
Not longing for that of wanting more
More of everything, or I am bored

I should learn to stay still, and see with my heart
All that I have, a long time from the start
My eyes cannot detect nor can I fathom
I am like a swine given pearls and no better am I
For still I do not learn

The great tug of war, pulling me back and forth
To and fro I will go, until my mind is set
A decision I alone must make
I ask myself, what is at stake
What do I change, it is my mindset

Now I Rise

Before, as I lay flat, less I could do
Then as I began to rise, much more could I
Like an empty cup and sometimes half full
When days of leisure were mine to behold

But when I am really empty, that's when it works best
I seem ready then, to move up and not rest
More thoughts driving through, and others
Thinking them too, I should myself be more

Double for your trouble, or tenfold from you
I was less, now I rise, your hands building me too
So looking down, now I see where I've been
And why, was meant to be

Happy and better off still, because you raised me
Though I only seem to be just a parking lot to many
To you I am your creation, look now what I can do
I hold so much more, my sign says, because of you

New Headstands

When I was much, much younger
On my head I loved to stand
I got a real kick out of it
Showing my upside down trick

And I did this well into my second score
Until one day my back no more
Suddenly an attack covered the display
The play I once did most every day

These days, still I can do much
Just not the splits and bending back
My thoughts and words in white and black
They have taken over that

You should see these new acrobats
With gracefulness like time last
The stir these words create, they attach
With metaphor and rhyme and some chat

I call them my new headstands
For more play they give to me
Sharing is now ever better more
Tremendously more can see

Growth and Transition

When you can see yourself clearly
in that new position
That big picture, the bird's eye view
It means that able are you to exchange your shoe
You have grown

When you shake the hand of someone new
Out of your comfort zone you start blooming too
Excited not shy, for now you are the confident you
You have grown

When you know you can do it
before you have done it
But grateful and humble you remain
You are a gift, it is their gain
You have grown

When you accept disappointments with grace
Your character will save your face
Remember, you are above the petty politics
You have grown

And now you are nearing transition
Or is it that you have already been doing it
Constantly growing is transition,
not physical but mental
Making ready, to be ready....you have grown

Rolling with the Punches

I can recall of some who can
Can roll with the punches
Ali, in the boxing ring, he took some hits
Though came out, with collateral damage

But ones of most significant memory
Were those, whose lives impacted me
Like my parents, some friends and family
Who stood by each other through difficulties

If I were a king I would crown them
Their conduct, something to admire
Their ways to delight in
Their presence a true blessing

Rolling is no bed of roses, the later often said
But that's life, to bend and flex, live to survive
Accepting that which you can't change
And changing that which you can

I say roll, roll with the punches too
Set an example worth following, you can
Pull up those socks, and girdle in
And promise to fight as hard as you can

JO ANNE C. BLACKMAN

What about You

What did you do in your younger days
What kind of games did you play
Tell me about your headstand moves
The way you see them working out today

Well did you have moves of your own
Or when you reflect were they borrowed
Like living in a shadow, or
Did you decide to make them your own

Have you looked at their blue prints microscopically
So pleased with their journeys, you copy
Or should you dare to reconsider
The hollowness you may have to swallow

Well, if that's your resolve, there is no parable
You say you lead, but in fact you follow
And that's okay, depending on whom you look up to
Remembering it's not about you

Laughing Too

Laughter, laughter, he, he, he
You tickle me
That laughing bag
Your best pal, whenever you forget how

How to laugh again, I wonder how
And if I try, will it happen now
I bet that laughing bag with a friend
Might remedy this sharp bend

Yes, no shortage, no drought
Did you know
This laughter brew, sharing power
To change your mood...ha, ha, ha

JO ANNE C. BLACKMAN

Refuge Safe Place

Refuge, safe place, I call it home
For where else shall I go
Filled with soft tenderness
Filled with care, my refuge here

Still here I find love, the love I yearn
And after long days of toil and dread
I can always return to my refuge, my home
To give away the stressful day

This home I love where no harm transpires
Much play and rest and filling up I acquire
Like a ship in the harbour
I am home, again and again

All my life I find here safe
For me the best hiding place
Like a secret no one else knows
Refuge, safe place, I call it home

Sugar or Honey

Sugar or honey what shall it be
Honey you are good for me pure and true
Sugar, so sweet are you

Sugar or honey what shall it be
Honey with lime you cure me
Sugar so sweet on my lips and tongue too

Sugar or honey what shall it be
Honey you are the real deal
Sugar you deceit, my life steal

As tempting as sugar may be
I know, really it is poison for me
Honey it will be, hopefully

Isn't that the case
Honey gives life
And sugar takes...choose honey, honey

The Nature of Trees

Orange, green, yellow more too
Bringing in the fall
And those trees, leaves falling bring
While others remain still green

Evergreens, green they are
How wonderfully firm they stay
In full form, bracing harsh blistery winter days
Through all seasons living, look at me, they do relay

Others go completely bare
As if breathless, you may glance twice, then stare
Though, it's only that they rest
Like the butterfly from the cocoon
Preparing for spectacular bloom, repeating

Like clockwork, she springs in
And new buds peep, then burst through
With lawns thawing out, from melting snow
Green as ever, the Evers, waving still hello

They all know their role, Evers to stay
Others to come and go
This is their style as nature, her circle throws
And even in summer, if I had to choose one
From roots to top, I would say Ever, here I come

Wake Up

I see the clever trap
Look, for feet are in straps
A thief has slipped you in
May be stolen the win

Hands stretched out, eyes shut
Bamboozled is your mind
Feet blindly walking
In a direction backward pulling

Wake up, wake up, and let the poison lose
Be courageous you, stop and choose
Burst free, your feet must be
Use all your might and fight, please fight

Though it's all in the mind
Chained is your heart, your flesh
All because of fallen thoughts
Seek more of yourself, don't remain caught

Do you earnestly strive, on your part
From this demise to separate and depart
Or still of two minds
Living in both times

Forward on, left or right then
Or worse remain, strapped in, no, no
Choose and believe, don't cave, don't give in
Take the Compass, find the Anchor
And please, do let Him in

JO ANNE C. BLACKMAN

When Pigs Fly

It's when the impossible happens
When you find a way to step out in faith
When you imagine something else, a new you
For a real desire to mend the current state
If I can see them up there, why can't you relate
Pigs do fly

No one can make pigs fly for you
Make up your mind in solo do
Even with your inner most strength
It challenges a shift to the very core
In weakness it is His power you need more
Pigs do fly

You look up now, and all you see is sky
I look up and I see pigs, they fly
One day, when life suddenly occurs to you
And you look up, you shall see them too
This is my sincere wish for you
That's when pigs fly

All Things

How does a father make
An old thing new
In the eyes of his child
All things he can do

Like raising the handles and the seat of a bike
And making it to fit your size
Like using a knife to scrape burnt toast
And you would never have known

Like building a kite with imagination and skill
Scraps of paper and strips of cloth
Wood from a cocoyea broom
May be flour and water for glue
Now eyes wide in amazement, a kite for you

It lifts off being pulled along
And mounts the air with its reckless tail
Dancing and bellowing
This talking kite, his making
All things he can do

Poet Four

And out of the blue
Not the sky, although unexpectedly
A comfort and a surprize
The gift of poet four

Recalling though, the three prior
Had always the knack
And in a wonderful wonder
Suddenly here was number four

Bursting at the seams
Uncontrolled by any other Light
Applying only green
As in go, and not stopping in between

Words printed as they came
From naught to more and more, then some
Astounding, the rapid flow
Unexplainable, can't say I know

Now I do know, though
What happened, was a wonderful thing
Super flowing, abounding, lifesaving
My Poetry writing

About the Author

I AM A FRIEND OF GOD. I HAVE KNOWN MYSELF TO LOVE Him forever, still there is a lot of room left in my serving Him. This is some of my story.

Born a Trinidadian, I immigrated to Canada with my young family in the late 80's. As a teenager I suffered the loss of my beloved father, as a result forming a closer cherished relationship with my mother.

In between the time I came to Canada and now, my children have grown into adults. It was a huge sacrifice and I do hope they would appreciate the attempt made to improve their possibilities. We never asked anyone for anything, we maintained our independence and stood on our own feet. I obtained my first job in Canada after one month of landing, and maintained a career in banking until May 2013. It was a huge part of my identity. This income was a necessity in helping to provide for our family. For me, there was no time for any indulgences, just work and home, and if we were not too tired, then church on Sundays. Oh, how things have changed!

I wouldn't say it was boring, rather it was exciting to relocate from Trinidad although challenging to resettle and it was admittedly adventurous, I was madly in love and everything was possible. This is entirely another story. I believed even at that time God was with me. As a family, sometimes we were sad and lonely, missing home. No "Skype" existed back then and connecting to our homeland by phone was costly. Writing letters and sending postcards were common. With a growing family within a few years *by the grace of God* we were able to purchase our first home. I can repeat this statement, thinking of each challenge encountered over the years, *"by the grace of God"*. Really I tell you, it is all that matters. Through the chapters of my life, each year here and before whether celebrating or depressed, experiencing tragedy or hardship, raising a family or letting go, grieving, job loss or weight gain, dealing with stress, worry or accepting change, God's grace has been constant..... by design.

By Design

From the valley to the mountain
Holding on to even the leg of that pig
That flying pig

Step by step
One day at a time
Reaching for that high

Years passing, like the blinking of an eye
And in the sinking of quick sand
God raising me each time

To belong to His tribe
Resurrection people
By design

———

Only recently did my writing start. Figuratively struck by lightning again and again, in a short space of time by September 2013, I felt devastated. Life happened. My world had crashed and about one year after, words like manna in the dessert, falling and filling me as I recognized and reflected on the sufficiency of God's grace.

A series of unfortunate circumstances, lent credit in that it allowed me the time to join a Small Group where we prayed and shared Scripture readings weekly, giving me that urgently needed light at the end of the tunnel. Even better I became part of a church community. I attended Sunday services, missing nearly none and became actively involved. I am now a lector at my church and intend to remain a full participant as God leads me in His purpose.

I did not think I would be able to make it through the ordeal of events which accelerated one after the other. I learned continually that my God loves me. He rescued me. I

JO ANNE C. BLACKMAN

survived in changing seasons because of Him, in my journey of faith with my identity switched and now in Christ. This is my testimony.

Jo Anne C. Blackman